HUNTERS
of the Night

Elaine Landau

WORDS TO KNOW

binocular vision—The ability to focus both eyes on an object at once.

camouflage—The use of an animal's coloring to blend in with its surroundings.

carnivores—Meat eaters.

colonies—Groups of animals that live together.

echolation—The process through which bats use sound to identify objects at night.

hibernate—To sleep deeply through the winter.

Jacobson's organ—An organ in a snake that can sense some chemicals released by a nearby animal.

mammal—An animal that has a warm body temperature. Mammal babies feed on their mothers' milk.

nocturnal—Active at night.

pollen—Tiny grains from flowering plants that are needed for these plants to reproduce, or make new plants.

predator—An animal that kills other animals for food.

prey—An animal that is hunted for food.

raptor—A bird with strong legs, powerful feet, and sharp claws.

reptiles—Animals that have backbones and lungs and are usually covered with scales. Also, their body temperatures adjust to the areas they are in.

venomous—Poisonous.

Raccoons can be very fierce.

Raccoons can easily see
a person in the dark.

NIGHT LIFE

Raccoons are nocturnal. They rest during the day and are active at night. Their bodies are good for night life. Raccoons hear well. This helps them find prey after dark. It is also useful in avoiding predators. They can hear an enemy come near them.

HUNTING AND EATING

Though they are called carnivores, raccoons are really omnivores. This means they will eat both animals and plants. They eat turtle eggs, bird eggs, berries, nuts, and insects. They have also been known to grab food from bird feeders, farmers' fields, and garbage bags.

Raccoons really enjoy crayfish, frogs, clams, and mussels they find in shallow waters. Raccoons feel for their prey in the water with their front paws. Wherever they get their food, raccoons dunk it in water before eating it.

This raccoon dips food in a stream in Oklahoma.

A hole in a tree can be a very safe place for a raccoon.

WHERE THE RACCOONS ARE

Raccoons' homes include hollow trees as well as burrows, or holes in the ground, left by other animals. Raccoons also live in brush piles, haystacks, caves, mines, or empty buildings.

In towns and cities, these wild animals often live very close to humans. They may be found in chimneys, sewers, under decks, or in people's attics. They often look for food in garbage cans. They tip over the cans and search for a tasty surprise inside.

PREDATORS

Raccoons in the wild have enemies. Coyotes, bobcats, and wolves eat them. Large owls, foxes, and badgers go after raccoon babies. Their mothers try to protect them, but sometimes raccoon babies are killed. Raccoons can live up to ten years in the wild.

These raccoon babies sleep safely away from predators.

RAISING YOUNG

Raccoon babies do not know how to climb trees at first. Their mothers have to teach them.

Young raccoons are helpless when they are born. They are born without teeth and with their eyes shut. Raccoon babies have hardly any fur. They depend on their mother for everything.

The young raccoons can stand when they are a little more than a month old. But their mother does not take them out of the den until they are three or four months old. They stay with their mother for about the first year of their lives. After that, they are on their own.

FUN FACTS ABOUT RACCOONS

★ Raccoons are at least as smart as dogs and cats.

★ Because raccoons are night animals, few people hear the sounds they make. But raccoons hiss, whistle, scream, and growl.

★ A raccoon can easily lift a dime out of a shirt pocket with its fingers.

★ The heaviest raccoon weighed sixty-two pounds.

★ The oldest raccoon lived for twenty-one years.

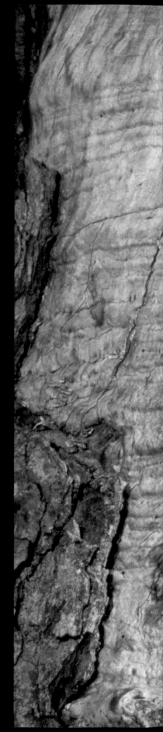

Raccoons stay safe in trees.

A leopard lets out
a mighty roar.

24

A LOOK AT BIG CATS

Scientists often say big cats are cats that roar. Only four cats do that—lions, tigers, leopards, and jaguars. This group of animals is called *Panthera* (PAN thair uh).

Big cats have more in common than their roar. All big cats are very large. A male lion can be about nine feet long from head to tail. A tiger can weigh five hundred pounds, or about as much as sixty house cats!

Big cats belong to a group of mammals called carnivores. Carnivores have special teeth for cutting meat. Big cats have powerful jaws and razor-sharp claws. Their four long, pointed front teeth are called canines. These help hold their prey.

A female leopard guards her prey.

HUNTERS OF THE NIGHT

Big cats are good hunters. Some stalk or quietly follow their victim from a distance. Others wait in hiding for an animal. Then they jump on their prey. They quickly pull it to the ground.

Lions, leopards, and tigers usually bite the animal's throat. This crushes its neck so it cannot breathe. Jaguars most often bite their prey's skull to kill it.

Big cats often drag their dead prey to a private spot. Leopards and jaguars sometimes drag their victims up a tree. There they can enjoy their meal without other animals trying to steal their food.

WHERE THE BIG CATS LIVE

A male and female lion finish their daytime rest as the sun sets. The lions are in the grasslands of Kenya, a country in Africa.

Lions and leopards live in Africa and Asia. Leopards live in forests, grasslands, mountains, and deserts. Lions, on the other hand, mostly live in grassy plains called savannas. They also live in open woodlands.

Tigers are only found in Asia. However, these animals can live in lots of different places. There are tigers in the freezing cold areas of Siberia as well as in hot rain forests.

Jaguars are the only big cats in the Americas. They mostly live near water in rain forests and swampy grasslands.

STAYING ALIVE

For the most part, big cats have no enemies in the wild. However, at times, male lions kill the cubs of other males. This can happen when a new male takes over a pride.

Tigers do not live in groups. But male tigers will also sometimes kill the cubs of other males.

Humans are the greatest danger to big cats. Hunting these cats is against the law in many places. However, these laws are not always obeyed.

Big cats, such as this jaguar, need to be protected from harm.

RAISING YOUNG

Big cats are helpless at birth. They drink their mother's milk for their first few months. During this time, their mother also keeps them safe. Young cubs are easy prey for larger animals.

Usually two to three cubs are born. But sometimes there may be as many as five or six. As the cubs get older, they watch their mother hunt. During this time, the playful cubs practice stalking small birds and insects.

After about two years, big cats begin to hunt alone. At this point, they are ready to live on their own.

A leopard cub learns to hunt by watching its mother.

33

Tigers like to attack their prey from behind.

34

FUN FACTS ABOUT BIG CATS

★ The African lion spends up to twenty hours a day sleeping or resting.

★ A tiger can eat about forty pounds of meat in a meal.

★ A leopard's spots are like a person's fingerprints. No two leopards have exactly the same pattern.

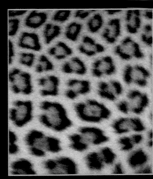

★ The lion is called the king of the jungle, but it lives in open grasslands.

★ Tigers only live in Asia. There are no tigers in Africa.

★ Tigers do not like to attack from the front. To avoid being attacked by tigers, jungle workers wear face masks on the backs of their heads. That way, a tiger always thinks the person is facing it.

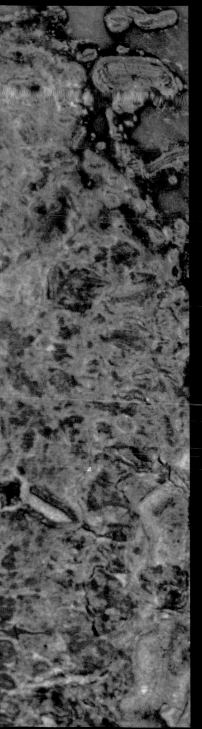

A LOOK AT OWLS

Though owls are birds, they are the same as humans in some ways. They sit upright. Owls also have eyes in the same place as those of people. Owls look straight ahead. They seem to stare at you. Most other birds have eyes on the sides of their heads.

Different owls have different calls. Not all sound like they are saying "whoo" or "hoot." Some owls make a barking sound. Others hiss, whistle, snort, or screech. The barred owl's call sounds like "Who cooks for you?"

Unlike other birds, owls have eyes on the front of their heads. This elf owl looks out from a tree.

READY FOR NIGHT LIFE

The soft tips of this eastern screech owl's wings help it fly silently through the night.

Owls can pick up sounds that people cannot hear. This helps them hunt the animals they eat after dark. An owl can hear a mouse running in the leaves more than twenty yards away.

Most owls can also see well even in dim light. Unlike most birds, owls have binocular vision. They can focus both eyes on an object at once. This helps them see how near their prey is. But owls can't turn their heads completely around.

Not only do many animals not see owls at night, they also do not hear them. Owls have feathers with soft tips. Birds with feathers that have hard tips make a swooshing sound in flight. But an owl's prey will not hear the owl coming because of its feathers' soft tips.

HUNTING AND EATING

Owls eat many different kinds of food. The largest owls hunt hares, squirrels, large birds, and other animals. Smaller owls live mostly on insects, frogs, lizards, and mice.

Owls are raptors. These are birds that eat other animals. All raptors have extremely strong legs and powerful feet. Owls also have razor-sharp claws called talons.

This tawny owl carries a mouse in its beak. The owl will feed its babies with the mouse.

The talons are used to grasp and kill prey. Owls often also use their talons to carry their prey through the air.

Owls do not chew their food. Small prey is swallowed whole. Owls use their beaks and talons to tear up larger prey. These pieces are swallowed without being chewed as well.

The prey's bones, teeth, claws, and feathers are coughed up in small, hard balls, called pellets. Scientists study these pellets to learn more about what owls eat.

A great horned owl in Arizona makes its nest in a cactus.

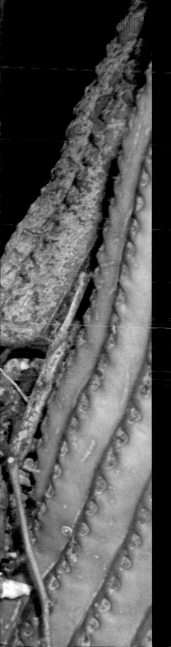

WHERE THE OWLS ARE

Owls live on every continent but Antarctica. Owls can be found in very cold places as well as in hot deserts. Many live in forests or wooded areas. Owls are also found on farmlands and grasslands.

Not all owls nest in trees. Burrowing owls nest underground. They use the old burrows of ground squirrels and other small animals.

Most owls tend to stay far away from humans. But barn owls and screech owls sometimes live in barns, church steeples, and other buildings.

OWL ENEMIES

Larger adult owls have few predators, or animals that eat them. But, when they are young, they are in more danger. Other animals eat them while they are young.

Smaller owls have many enemies. Larger owls, coyotes, weasels, hawks, raccoons, and other animals eat them. An owl's coloring often helps hide it. This is known as camouflage.

Some owls' brown and gray feathers blend in well with tree bark. It is hard to spot one roosting in a tree. The mostly white snowy owl lives in open areas as far north as the Arctic. Its white feathers make it hard to spot as well.

The snowy owl blends in well with its snowy home.

RAISING YOUNG

Young owl chicks are helpless. They are blind at birth and have only a thin layer of down, or feathers, for warmth. They need their mother's care to stay alive.

The mother owl feeds her chicks and protects them from predators. Father owls bring back food for the family, too.

The chicks learn to hunt and to fly while with their parents. After about two or three months, they are ready to leave the nest.

Baby screech owls have fluffier feathers than their parents.

FUN FACTS ABOUT OWLS

★ Female owls are usually bigger than males. Some scientists think they are bigger so they can protect the nest. Others believe that females need to catch larger prey than males.

★ An owl has a lot of feathers on its legs and feet. This is to protect it from snake and rat bites.

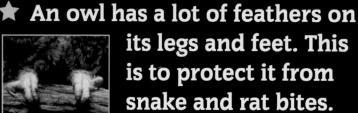

★ Owls are not the "wisest" birds. Parrots as well as some other birds are smarter.

★ It is illegal to own an owl as a pet in the United States.

★ Owl mummies have been found in the tombs of ancient Egyptian rulers.

★ Barn owls are better at catching mice than cats are. A family of barn owls will eat about thirteen hundred mice a year.

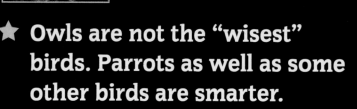

★ Barn owls are sometimes called "monkey-faced owls" because of their white heart-shaped faces and dark eyes.

Some people
think barn owls'
faces look like
those of monkeys.

49

A LOOK AT BATS

Bats are divided into two main groups, mega bats and micro bats.

Mega bats are medium- to large-sized bats. Most have long doglike snouts, large eyes, and small ears. They mostly live in tropical places in Australia, Africa, and Asia. Flying foxes are the largest mega bats.

Micro bats are the other group of bats. Most of these bats are smaller than mega bats. Their faces look different too. There are more kinds of micro bats than mega bats. Micro bats can be found throughout much of the world. The world's smallest micro bat is the hog-nosed bat from Thailand.

This flying fox bat in
Australia has a snout
like a dog's and a
face like a fox's.
It is a mega bat.

Look how small the
bumblebee bat is!
It is a micro bat.

FEEDING TIME!

Though many bats eat insects, not all bats are meat eaters. Many mega bats eat fruits, such as mangoes and bananas. Others use their long snouts to lap up nectar from flowers.

Some micro bats also eat fruit, but most eat insects. They eat flies, mosquitoes, beetles, spiders, and cockroaches. A few kinds of bats eat fish, frogs, scorpions, small birds, lizards, and rats.

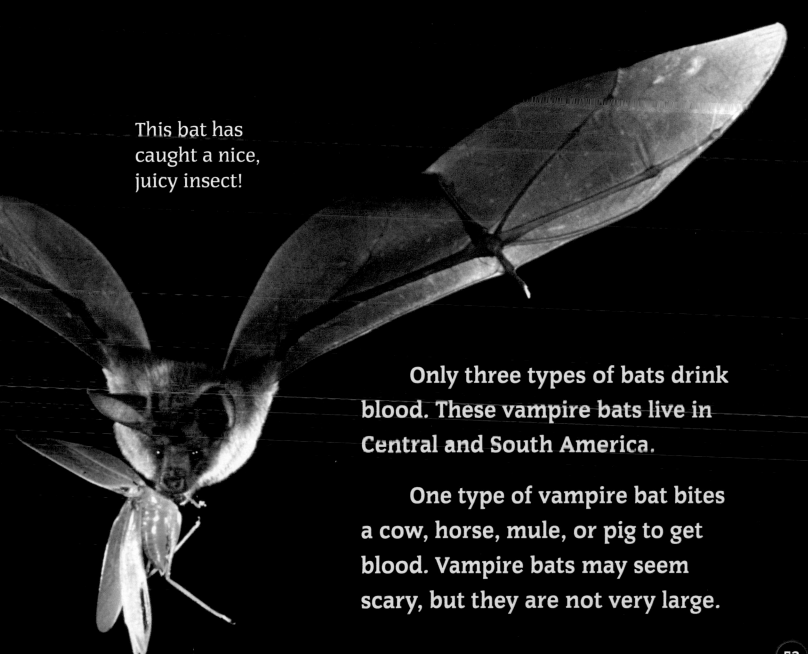

This bat has caught a nice, juicy insect!

Only three types of bats drink blood. These vampire bats live in Central and South America.

One type of vampire bat bites a cow, horse, mule, or pig to get blood. Vampire bats may seem scary, but they are not very large.

THE BAT CAVE AND MORE

Some bats live in caves, but others can be found in old mines, trees, bridges, and cracks in rock. They live in forests, fields, and near lakes, ponds, and streams. Bats are even found in cities.

Many bats live together in colonies. A large colony can have millions of bats. The world's largest bat colony is in Bracken Cave in Texas. During the summers, as many as 20 million Mexican free-tailed bats may roost there.

Other bats live by themselves. Many more live in pairs.

In the winter, some bats migrate, or travel, to warmer places. Others hibernate, spending the winter in a deep sleep.

A vampire-bat colony on a tree trunk.

A ghost bat comes out of hiding at night to hunt.

STAYING ALIVE

There are few animals that eat bats in the wild. At times, predators like hawks, snakes, and cats eat them. Yet bats are often able to avoid these animals. During the day, they roost, or sit and rest, in high or hidden places where many animals cannot get to them.

As a result, bats live longer than many mammals their size. Some types of bats live for more than twenty years.

BAT BABIES

Bat babies are called pups. Usually bats have one pup at a time. Yet some types of bats may have two or even four pups. Like all mammals, mother bats nurse, or feed their pups milk. Mother bats can always find their pups out of thousands in a roost. They know their pups by their cry and how they smell.

A Gambian bat holds her pup tightly as they both hang upside down.

This bat is eating fruit from the Saguaro cactus plant.

HOW BATS HELP

Bats are helpful to humans. Micro bats eat harmful insects. Many of these insects destroy crops and spread disease.

Bats that drink nectar, a sweet fluid produced by flowers, are important, too. As these bats sip a flower's nectar, pollen collects on their fur. When they fly to other flowers, they spread the pollen. This lets new plants grow.

Fruit-eating bats are needed as well. These bats drop fruit seeds as they eat. The seeds grow into new plants.

Bat droppings, called guano (GWAH noh), also contain seeds that grow. Bat guano is useful to farmers, too. It is an excellent fertilizer for their crops.

Vampire bats feed on the blood of other animals.

FUN FACTS ABOUT BATS

★ Bat guano is rich in nitrogen (NY truh jen)—a colorless, odorless gas. That makes it a good fertilizer for farming.

★ Have you ever heard the saying, "Blind as a bat?" Bats are not blind. Some have very good eyesight.

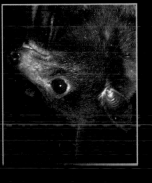

★ A bat can find an insect up to eighteen feet away using echolocation (eh koh loh KAY shun).

★ Bats can carry rabies. This disease can be passed from bats and other mammals to people. If someone with rabies is not treated quickly, that person will die. Very few bats ever get rabies.

★ Vampire bats are the only mammals that live entirely on blood.

★ Some types of bats will bring food to an ill bat that cannot hunt. Female bats have also cared for bat babies whose mothers have died.

A reticulated python

A LOOK AT BIG SNAKES

There are almost three thousand types of snakes in the world. Some are venomous (VEH nuh mus), or poisonous, though most snakes are not.

Some snakes are small, while others are very large. The reticulated (reh TIH kyoo lay ted) python can grow to more than forty-five feet long. That is the length of a bus! The green anaconda can weigh more than four hundred pounds!

NIGHT HUNTING

Snakes are good night hunters. They do not use sight and hearing the way people do.

A snake has a forked, or split, tongue. The snake flicks out its tongue. When its tongue goes back into its mouth, it touches the snake's Jacobson's organ. This body part senses the taste and smell of a nearby animal. It lets the snake know that a meal is close.

Snakes also use nostrils to pick up stronger scents and those coming from far away. Snakes sometimes place their jaws on the ground to feel the other animals' movements as well.

Some snakes, such as pit vipers, have special organs for hunting after dark. These are pits on each side of the snake's head that sense the heat of prey.

A white-lipped viper's pits are above its mouth. This viper shows its forked tongue, too.

WHERE THE BIG SNAKES ARE

Most big snakes live where the weather is warm. They are found in fields and forests, on rocky hillsides, underground, and in wetlands.

Cottonmouth snakes are mostly found in wetlands in the southeastern United States. Other big snakes live in grasslands and deserts. Rattlesnakes live in deserts and forests from Canada to South America. Many are in the United States.

Still other snakes live in trees, caves, or in fresh or salt water. Many boa constrictors are good climbers. They are often spotted in rain forests. In some places, snakes are also found in towns and cities.

The cottonmouth snake spends time in the water. Cottonmouths are also called water moccasins.

STAYING ALIVE

The color and design of a snake's scales help it stay alive. Brown or grayish rattlesnakes match the ground and rocks. Copperhead snakes have wide reddish-brown bands to match logs. Predators cannot easily see them. This is known as camouflage.

Poisonous snakes are often brightly colored. Their bright colors warn predators to stay away. Other snakes scare off predators by lifting their heads up high or thrashing about. When a cobra is angry, a piece of loose skin called a hood flares out behind its head.

Snakes also use sounds as a defense. Some snakes hiss. Rattlesnakes shake rattles at the ends of their tails.

Still other snakes break off their tail if a predator has grabbed it. A new tail grows back to replace it.

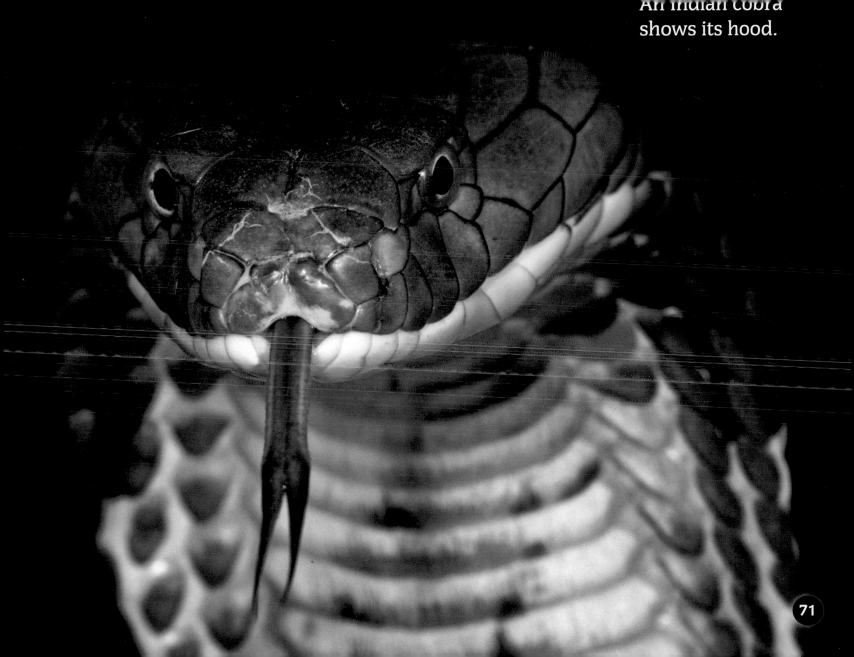

An Indian cobra
shows its hood.

71

A baby green mamba breaks out of its egg.

However, some types of female snakes stay to protect their eggs from predators.

Other snakes give birth to live young. Among these are rattlesnakes and garter snakes. The first year of a young snake's life is very dangerous. Many are eaten by crows, skunks, snapping turtles, baboons, and other animals, including other snakes.

HOW SNAKES MOVE

Snakes do not have legs or feet. Yet they move with ease. Here are the three main ways snakes move:

The S-shaped Wave

Here the snake uses its muscles to curve its body. It looks something like the letter S. The curves of the snake's body push against the ground. This moves the snake forward in a wavy path.

The Belly Crawl

Larger, heavier snakes move this way. These snakes push down on their belly scales and slide forward. They move ahead in a nearly straight line.

Side Winding

Snakes that live on sand move forward by lifting the main part of its body and thrusting it forward sideways. Then it moves its head and tail up to the rest of its body. The sidewinder rattlesnake moves this way.

These pythons make the letter "S" with their bodies when they move.

A boa constrictor kills a mouse by squeezing it. Then, it swallows the mouse whole.

FUN FACTS ABOUT BIG SNAKES

★ A cobra's biggest enemy is the mongoose. A mongoose is only about  sixteen inches long but is very fast. When it attacks a cobra, it almost always kills it.

★ The biggest snake ever captured is a forty-nine-foot python. It is on display at a park in Indonesia.

★ Wearing boots that cover the ankle could stop about 25 percent of all snakebites.

★ The oldest snake in a zoo was a boa constrictor named Popeye from the Philadelphia Zoo. It lived for more than forty years.

★ Snake teeth usually point backward toward its throat. That keeps a snake's prey from getting away.

A LOOK AT ALLIGATORS AND CROCS

Both alligators and crocodiles have sharp, pointed teeth. The teeth on a crocodile's lower jaw show when its mouth is closed.

Crocodiles are more likely to attack than alligators.

Alligators and crocodiles are reptiles. Their body temperature does not stay the same. It changes to match the area they are in. On cool mornings, they often rest in the sun. This heats them up. When it gets too hot, they cool off in the water.

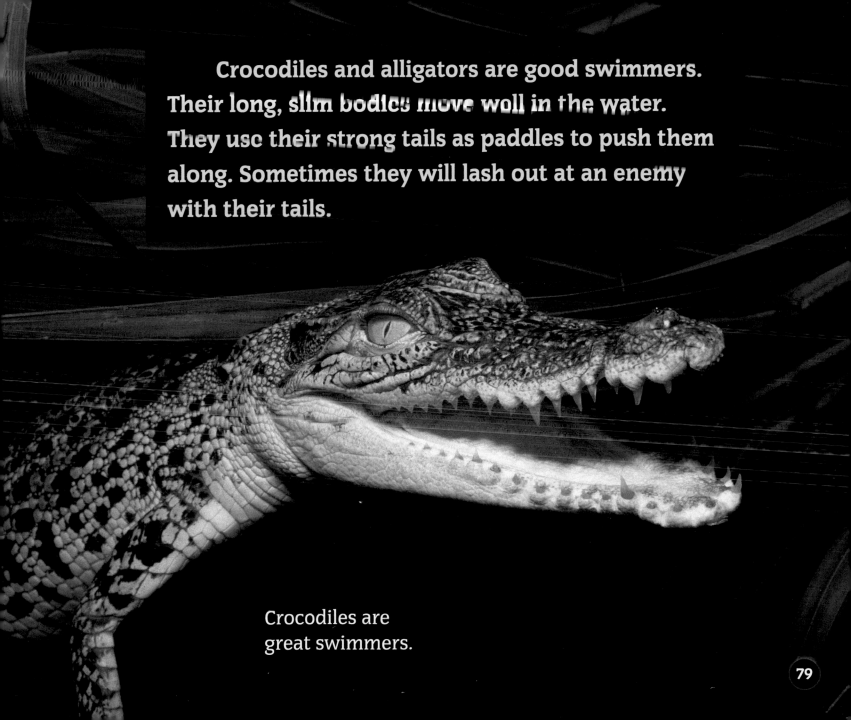

Crocodiles and alligators are good swimmers.
Their long, slim bodies move well in the water.
They use their strong tails as paddles to push them
along. Sometimes they will lash out at an enemy
with their tails.

Crocodiles are
great swimmers.

MADE FOR NIGHT LIFE

You can see crocodiles and alligators during the day. They often rest in the sun. But they move around more at night.

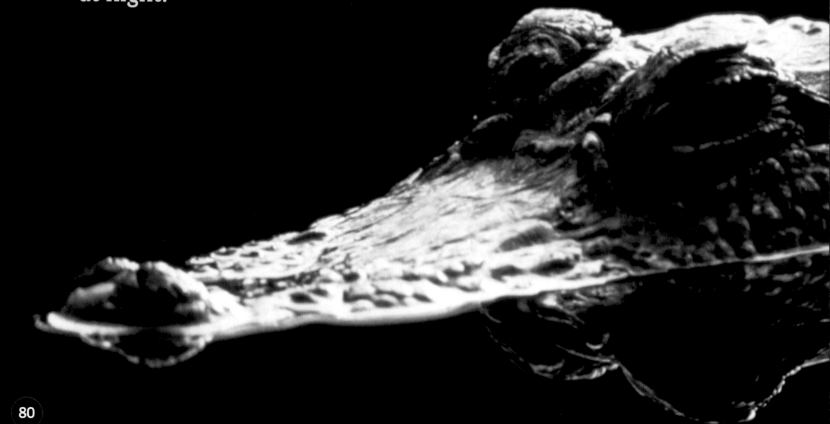

Crocodiles and alligators see well in the dark. They can spot prey that might not see them. They can also smell and hear nearby animals after dark. These reptiles do not need daylight to find a meal.

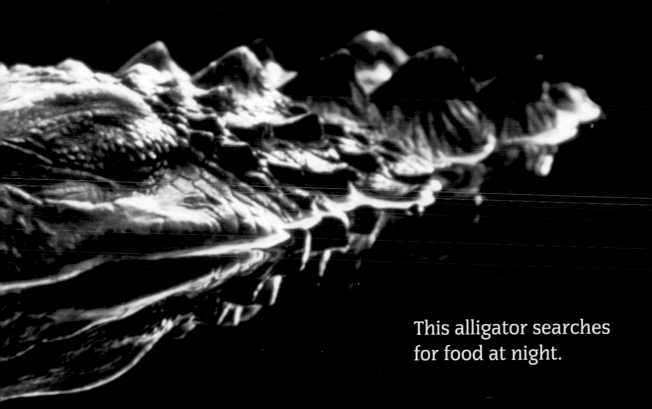

This alligator searches for food at night.

LATE NIGHT SNACKING

Eating larger prey takes more work. Crocodiles and alligators twist and pull their prey's body until smaller chunks break off. These pieces are swallowed in one gulp. Crocodiles and alligators throw back their heads while swallowing. This makes the food fall down their throats.

Crocodiles and alligators are meat eaters. Smaller alligators and crocodiles usually eat fish, turtles, birds, and frogs. Bigger ones eat monkeys, oxen, pigs, deer, antelope, and other large animals.

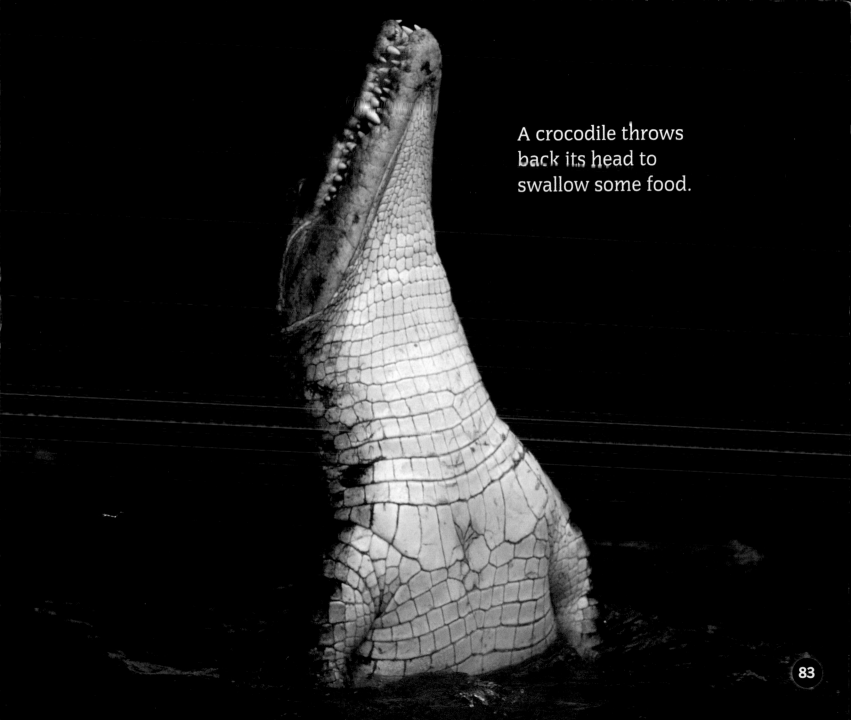

A crocodile throws back its head to swallow some food.

HOME SWEET HOME

Crocodiles and alligators live in places where the weather is warm. This is especially true of crocodiles. They are in the hottest parts of Africa, Australia, Southeast Asia, and North and South America.

American alligators mostly live in the southeastern United States. They are in Alabama, Arkansas, North and South Carolina, Florida, Georgia, Louisiana, Mississippi, Oklahoma, and Texas.

Alligators live in fresh water. They are found in swamps, marshes, ponds, lakes, and some rivers.

Some species or types of crocodiles live in salty waters near the ocean. There are also freshwater crocodiles. These are found in swamps, lakes, and other freshwater spots. Others live in both salt water and fresh water.

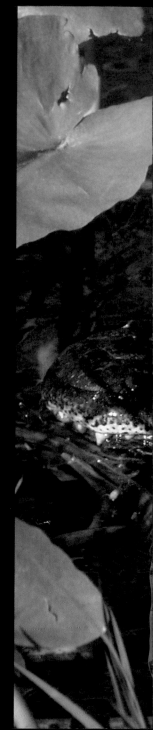

This alligator lives
in a swamp.

Baby alligators can be easily eaten by other animals because they are so small and cannot fight back as well as adult alligators.

STAYING ALIVE

Adult crocodiles and alligators do not have many predators. Few other animals are as large and strong. However, large snakes in Asia have attacked crocodiles. Lately, big snakes have attacked alligators in Florida.

Crocodiles and alligators have also been killed while hunting. Crocodiles sometimes attack the babies of big animals, such as elephants. If the mothers of these animals are nearby, they defend their babies. Crocodiles have died in these fights.

Very young crocodiles and alligators cannot defend themselves. Snakes, raccoons, turtles, and other animals eat them. Large crocodiles and alligators sometimes eat smaller ones as well.

An alligator moves eggs around her nest with her mouth.

RAISING BABIES

Like most reptiles, female crocodiles lay eggs. Some female crocodiles dig a hole in the sand. They lay their eggs there. Then they cover the eggs with sand. These make little hills, or mounds. Others build mound nests of soil, leaves, and twigs. Female alligators build mound nests, too.

The female lays her eggs in the center of the mound. Then she covers her eggs. She stays close by to guard the nest.

Female crocodiles and alligators stay with their babies for about two years. They carry them to the water in their mouths. They also try to protect them from predators.

STAYING SAFE

Now, in some areas, humans live fairly close to alligators and crocodiles. These animals do not usually look for people to attack. They have a natural fear of humans. It is best to keep it that way since they sometimes do attack if people get too close. If you live or visit where there are crocodiles or alligators, follow these tips:

- Stay away from crocodiles or alligators.

- Never throw anything at these reptiles or tease them.

- Do not feed these animals. It makes them lose their fear of humans.

- Do not swim where you know there are crocodiles or alligators.

- Crocodiles and alligators are wild animals. They can never be pets.

Crocodiles and alligators attack quickly. People should not get close to them.

This dwarf crocodile lives in Africa. It is smaller than other crocodiles.

FUN FACTS ABOUT ALLIGATORS AND CROCODILES

★ Ancient crocodile mummies have been found in Egypt.

★ The American alligator can stay underwater for up to two hours.

★ Crocodiles and alligators keep growing all their lives.

★ Crocodiles can go for months without eating. They live on the fat stored in their tails.

★ Crocodiles and alligators never run out of teeth. New teeth grow to replace those that fall out.

LEARN MORE

BOOKS

Gish, Melissa. *Alligators.* Mankato, Minn.: Creative Education, 2011.

Hurtig, Jennifer. *Raccoons.* New York: Weigl Publishers, 2008.

Kalman, Bobbie, and Kristina Lundblad. *Endangered Bats.* New York: Crabtree Pub., 2006.

Lynch, Wayne. *Owls.* Minnetonka, Minn.: NorthWord Press, 2005.

Markle, Sandra. *Snakes: Biggest! Littlest!* Honesdale, Pa.: Boyds Mills Press, 2005.

_____. *Crocodiles.* Minneapolis, Minn.: Carolrhoda Books, 2004.

Patent, Dorothy Hinshaw. *Big Cats.* New York: Walker & Co., 2005.

Simon, Seymour. *Snakes.* New York: HarperCollins, 2007.

Stefoff, Rebecca. *Lions.* New York: Marshall Cavendish Benchmark, 2006.

Taschek, Karen. *Hanging With Bats: Ecobats, Vampires, and Movie Stars.* Albuquerque: University of New Mexico Press, 2008.

Warhol, Tom. *Owls.* New York: Marshall Cavendish Benchmark, 2007.

LEARN MORE

INTERNET ADDRESSES

Animal Tracks. Raccoons.
<http://www.bear-tracker.com/coon.html>

National Geographic Kids. Videos—Night Owls.
<http://video.nationalgeographic.com/video/player/kids/animals-pets-kids/wild-detectives-kids/wd-ep2-owls.html>

Organization for Bat Conservation. For Kids.
<http://www.batconservation.org/drupal/bats-for-kids>

San Diego Zoo. Reptiles: Alligators and Crocodiles
<http://www.sandiegozoo.org/animalbytes/t-crocodile.html>

San Diego Zoo. Reptiles: Snakes!
<http://www.sandiegozoo.org/animalbytes/t-snake.html>

Wildlife Conservation Society. Big Cats.
<http://www.wcs.org/saving-wildlife/big-cats.aspx>

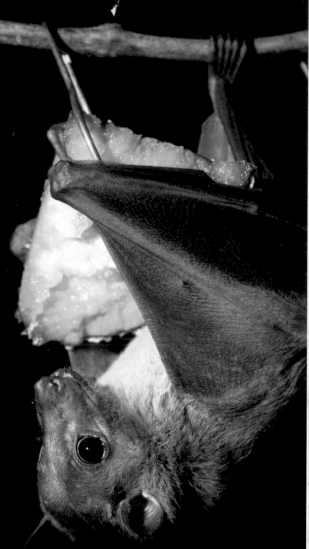

Library of Congress Cataloging-in-Publication Data

Landau, Elaine.

  Hunters of the night / Elaine Landau.

    p. cm.

  Summary: "Discover a variety of animals, such as owls, big cats, and bats, who hunt at night"—
Provided by publisher.

  ISBN 978-1-4644-0033-9

  1. Nocturnal animals—Juvenile literature. 2. Predatory animals—Juvenile literature. I. Title.

QL755.5.L375 2012

591.5'18—dc23

                    2011032132

Printed in China

082011 Leo Paper Group, Heshan City, Guangdong, China

10 9 8 7 6 5 4 3 2 1

To Our Readers: We have done our best to make sure all Internet Addresses in this book were active and appropriate when we went to press. However, the author and the publisher have no control over and assume no liability for the material available on those Internet sites or on other Web sites they may link to. Any comments or suggestions can be sent by e-mail to comments@enslow.com or to the address on the back cover.

Photo Credits: © 2011 Photos.com, a division of Getty Images, pp. 2 (reptile) 30, 35, 46–47, 48 (both), 77 (both), 93 (right), 96; Alamy: © Jeff Rotman, p. 79, © Rick & Nora Bowers, pp. 2 (owl), 36, 42, © WorldFoto, p. 28; © Gloria H. Chomica/Masterfile, p. 7; The Image Bank/Getty Images, p. 91; iStockphoto.com: © Marco Kopp, p. 24, © Mark Nelson, p. 34; © Leszczynski, Zigmund/Animals Animals - Earth Scenes, p. 69; © McDonald Wildlife Photog./Animals Animals - Earth Scenes, pp. 38, 64; Minden Pictures: © Anup Shah/NPL, p. 33, © Michael D. Kern/NPL, pp. 1 (cobra), 71, © Michael & Patricia Fogden, p. 62, © Stephen Dalton, pp. 40–41; National Geographic/Getty Images, pp. 86, 88; © NHPA/Photoshot, pp. 2 (snake), 67; © Photolibrary, pp. 1 (alligator, raccoon), 2 (bat), 19, 55; Photo Researchers, Inc.: Alan and Sandy Carey, p. 1 (jaguar), Anthony Bannister, p. 72, B. G. Thomson, pp. 1 (bat), 51 (flying fox bat), 56, Dante Fenolio, p. 92, Dr. Merlin D. Tuttle, pp. 51 (bumblebee bat), 52–53, 59, 60, Paul Whitten, p. 76, Phil A. Dotson, p. 15, Ray Coleman, p. 16, Steve Maslowski, pp. 2 (raccoon), 20–21, 23, William Ervin, p. 26; © Photoshot, pp. 80–81; Riser/Getty Images, p. 83; Shutterstock.com, pp. 1 (owl), 3, 11, 12, 22, 49, 63, 75, 85, 93 (left); © Tom Mangelsen/Naturepl.com, p. 45; U.S. Fish and Wildlife Service, p. 9; Visuals Unlimited/Getty Images, p. 4.

Cover Photos: © Michael D. Kern/NPL/ Minden Pictures (cobra); © Photolibrary (alligator, raccoon); Photo Researchers, Inc.: Alan and Sandy Carey (jaguar), B. G. Thomson (bat); Shutterstock.com (owl). **Back Cover:** © 2011 Photos.com, a division of Getty Images.

Literacy Advisor: Allan A. De Fina, PhD, Dean, College of Education/Professor of Literacy Education, New Jersey City University.

Enslow Elementary

an imprint of

Enslow Publishers, Inc.

E

40 Industrial Road
Box 398
Berkeley Heights, NJ 07922
USA

http://www.enslow.com